All About
DRAWING

Sea Creatures & Animals

Illustrated by Russell Farrell and Diana Fisher

Getting Started

When you **look** closely at the **drawings** in this book, you'll notice that they're made up of basic shapes, such as circles, triangles, and rectangles. To draw all your underwater and wild kingdom favorites, just start with simple shapes as you see here. It's easy and fun!

Circles
are used to draw eyes, heads, and round bodies.

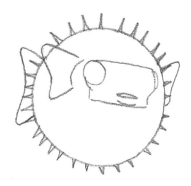

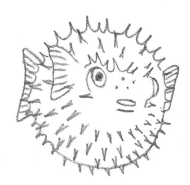

Ovals
are good for drawing animals' bodies.

Triangles
are best for drawing the heads of some fish.

FIND THE SHAPE!

Can you find a circle, an oval, and a triangle on this colorful toucan? Look closely at the beak, eye, and body. It's easy to see the basic shapes in any animal once you know what to look for!

Coloring Tips

There's more than one way to bring your **animal** friends to life on paper—you can use crayons, markers, or colored pencils. Just be sure you have plenty of good natural colors— blue, green, and brown, plus gray, yellow and orange.

Pencil

Colored pencil

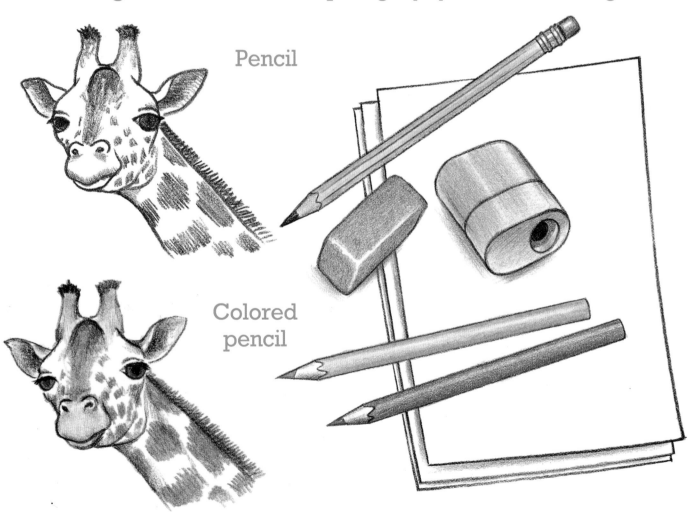

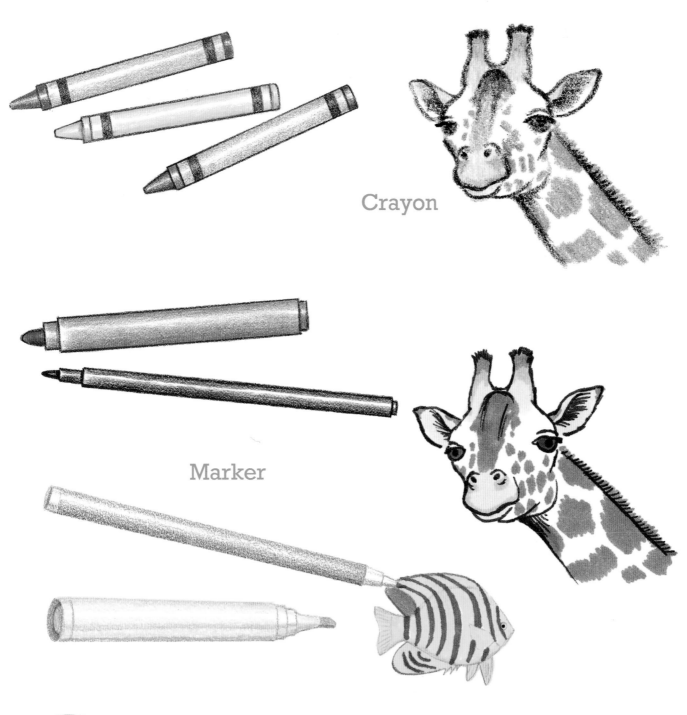

Crayon

Marker

With an assortment of creatures under the sea and on land, the color possibilities are endless! Before you pick a coloring tool for your drawing, think about the animal's different textures. Is its skin furry, feathered, scaled, or smooth? Colored pencils have a sharp tip that is great for tiny details like small hairs and feathers. Crayons can be used to cover large areas quickly and markers make your colors look smooth and solid.

Puffer

The body of the **puffer** is one of the **simplest** shapes of all sea creatures—its body is nearly a perfect circle!

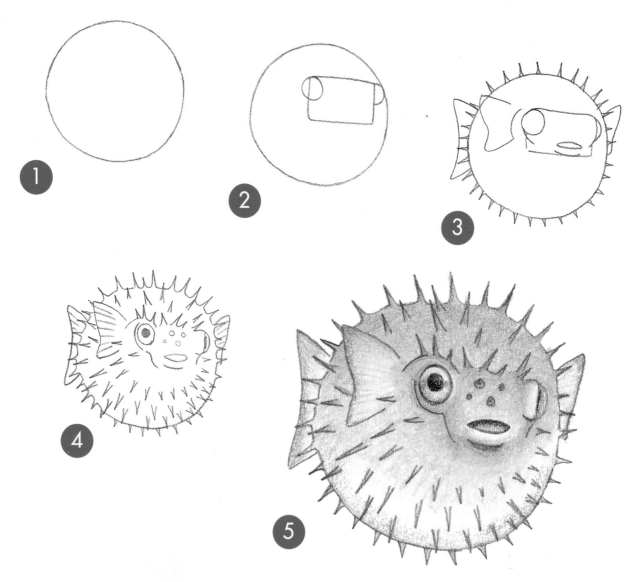

1

2

3

4

5

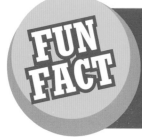

FUN FACT

With all the predators in the ocean, many fish have adapted unique ways to defend themselves. The puffer (also called the "blowfish" or "swellfish") can fill itself up with air or water to become a round, spiky ball, making it very difficult to swallow!

Aardvark

The aardvark has a **long** nose, **beady** eyes, and sharp claws. It first smells and then digs out its meals of ants and termites.

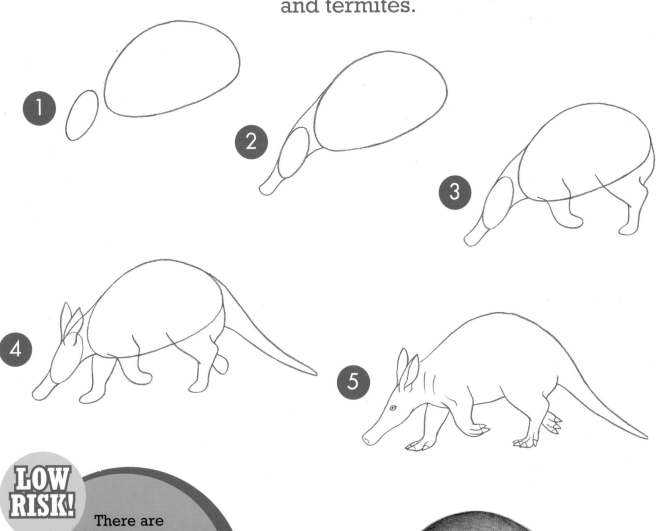

LOW RISK!

There are many aardvarks in the world today, so this animal is at low risk for extinction. *Extinct* means that none are left.

Angelfish

An **elegant** creature, this **tropical** fish is known for its vibrant stripes of color.

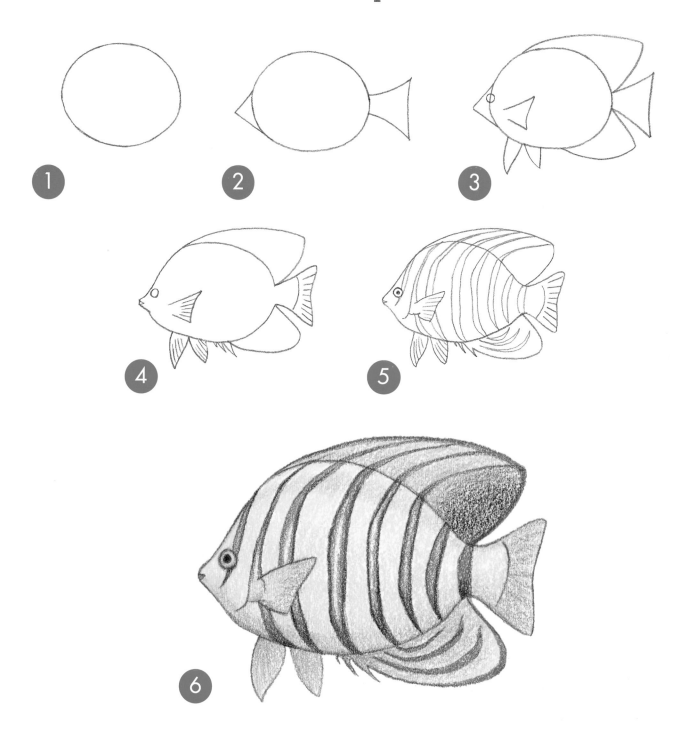

Emu

The emu's **fluffy** plumage hides its small **wings.** But its tall, thin legs allow this flightless bird to run up to 30 miles per hour!

FUN FACT

Some say the emu's name comes from Arabic or Aboriginal words for "large bird"; others say it mimics the male bird's call of "e-moo."

Giant Panda

In China the **barrel-shaped** panda is called "baixiong" ("white bear"), but the black markings give this animal a two-toned look.

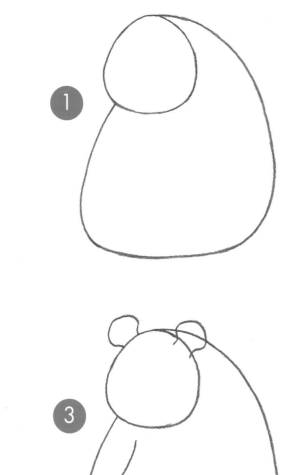

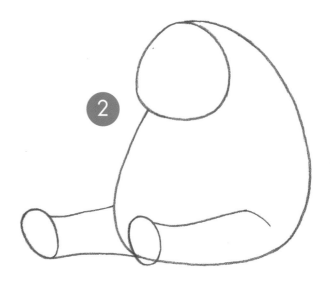

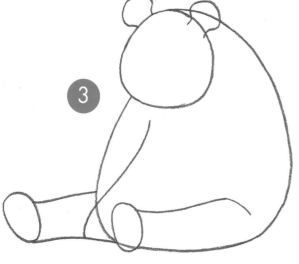

FUN FACT

The giant panda has a very limited diet—it survives almost entirely on bamboo! It eats the shoots of this grasslike plant in the spring, the leaves in the summer, and the stems in the winter.

Polar Bear

The cuddly polar bear has a **large,** round, **furry** body—but this cutie hunts and devours seals, walruses, and even whales!

5

Polar bears are so well insulated that sometimes they overheat and have to cool off in the icy water! They also spend a lot of time bathing after meals to keep their thick coats white fur clean.

Harp Seal

Draw this **sweet** baby harp seal with **rounded,** gently curving lines and big, dark, "puppy-dog" eyes.

A baby harp seal is born with thick white fur, but after 1-1/2 weeks it develops a gray-brown coat with darker, harp-shaped (or horseshoelike) patches.

Toucan
keel-billed

It's hard to ignore the **keel-billed** toucan's beak! It's almost as long as the bird's body—and it features a rainbow of colors.

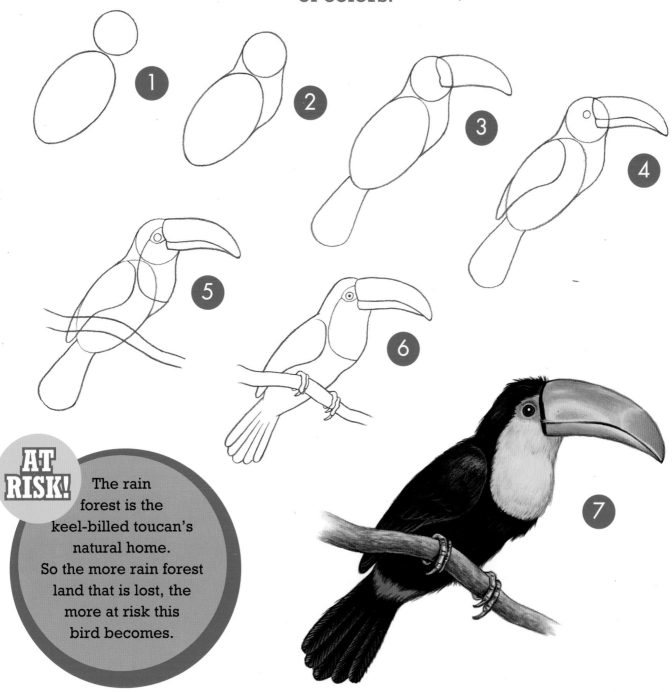

AT RISK! The rain forest is the keel-billed toucan's natural home. So the more rain forest land that is lost, the more at risk this bird becomes.

Cheetah

With its **long,** powerful legs; **lean,** muscular body; and stylish, spotted coat, you might say the cheetah is a hunter that's "dressed to kill"!

Unlike lions and tigers, cheetahs don't roar, but they do purr, growl, bark, and even make chirruping sounds!

5

6

Reaching speeds of more than 60 mph, the cheetah is the fastest animal in the world, but this big cat can maintain its top speed only for short bursts. After 10–12 seconds of running, the cheetah begins to overheat.

Humpback Whale

Weighing in at **2 tons,** the humpback is a **whale** of a creature—its huge fins are nearly 1/3 as long as its body!

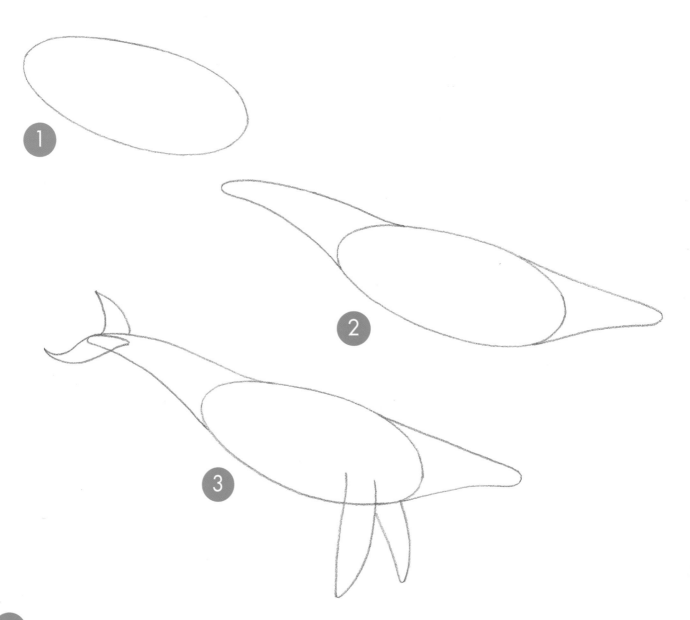

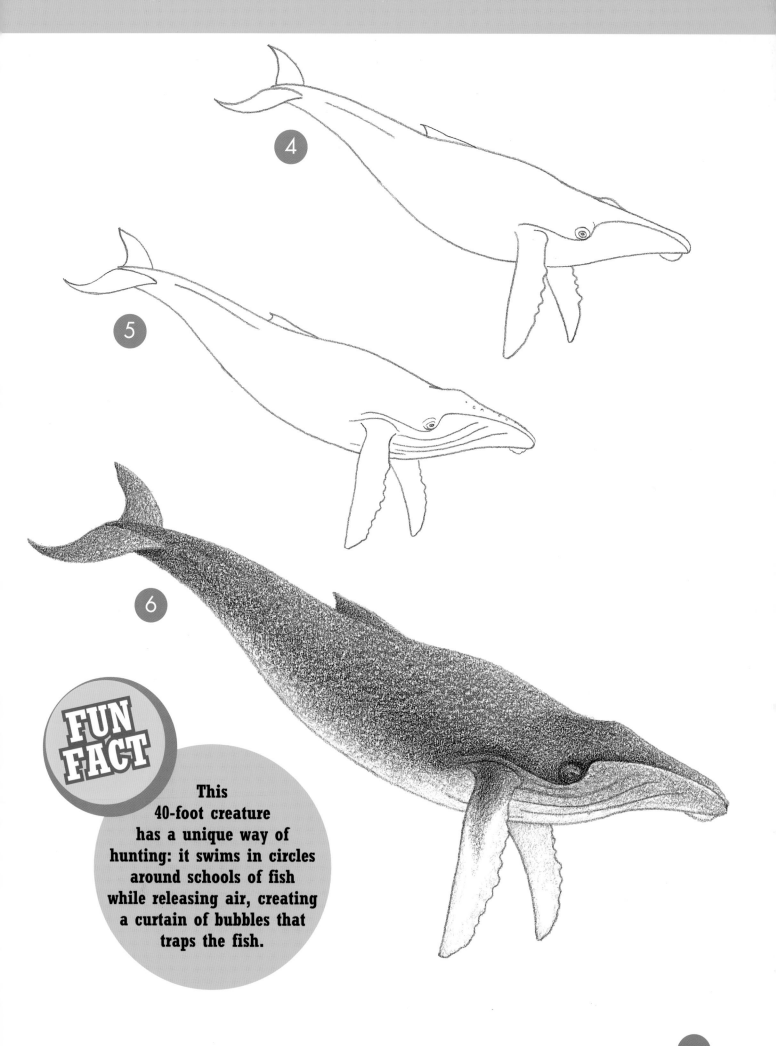

FUN FACT

This 40-foot creature has a unique way of hunting: it swims in circles around schools of fish while releasing air, creating a curtain of bubbles that traps the fish.

Sea Star

Start drawing this **sea** animal with simple **circles!**
Then add five triangular arms to create the star shape.

1

2

3

4

5

Wildebeest

The wildebeest—or gnu—looks **big** and **broad** with high shoulders and a humped back, but it prances away from danger on four skinny legs!

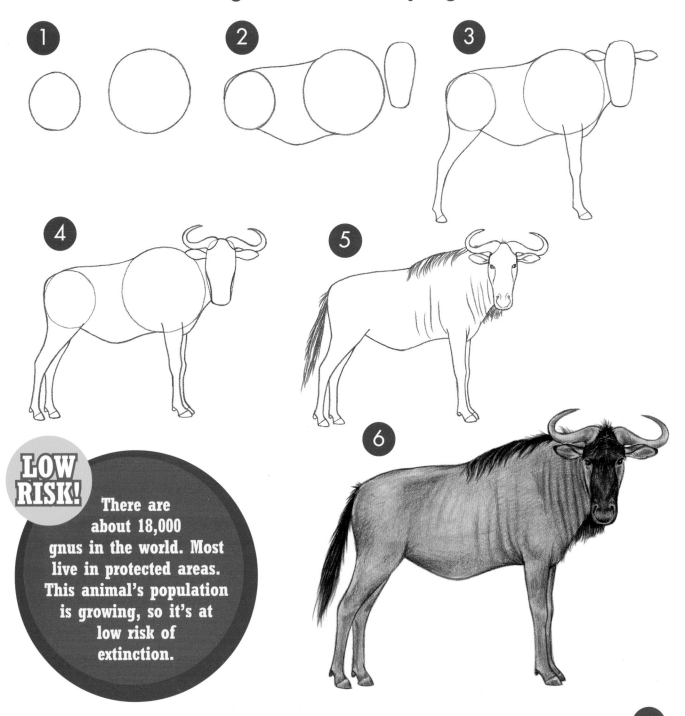

1

2

3

4

5

6

LOW RISK!

There are about 18,000 gnus in the world. Most live in protected areas. This animal's population is growing, so it's at low risk of extinction.

Elephant

One of the **largest** beasts of the **animal** kingdom, an African elephant has a thick trunk, big legs, long tusks, and giant ears!

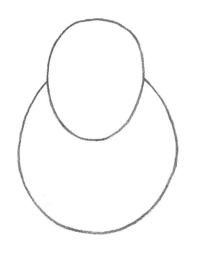

1

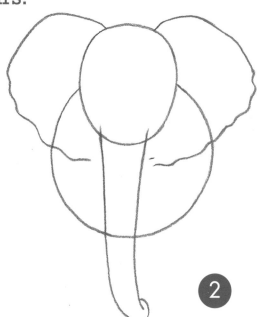

2

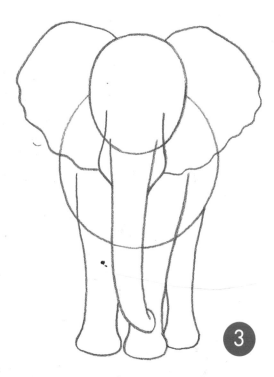

3

4

⑤

⑥

The elephant is known for its great memory—but why? One reason is the elephant has an enormous brain! Weighing in at around 12 pounds, it's the largest and heaviest mammal brain. (The human brain weighs only about 3 pounds.)

Great White Shark

The most **feared** of all sharks, this **predator** has a long, pointed snout and razor-sharp, triangular teeth.

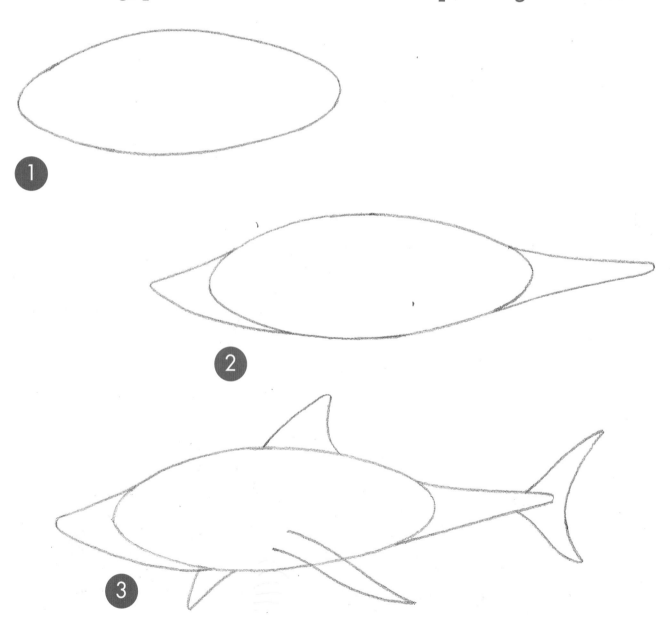

1

2

3

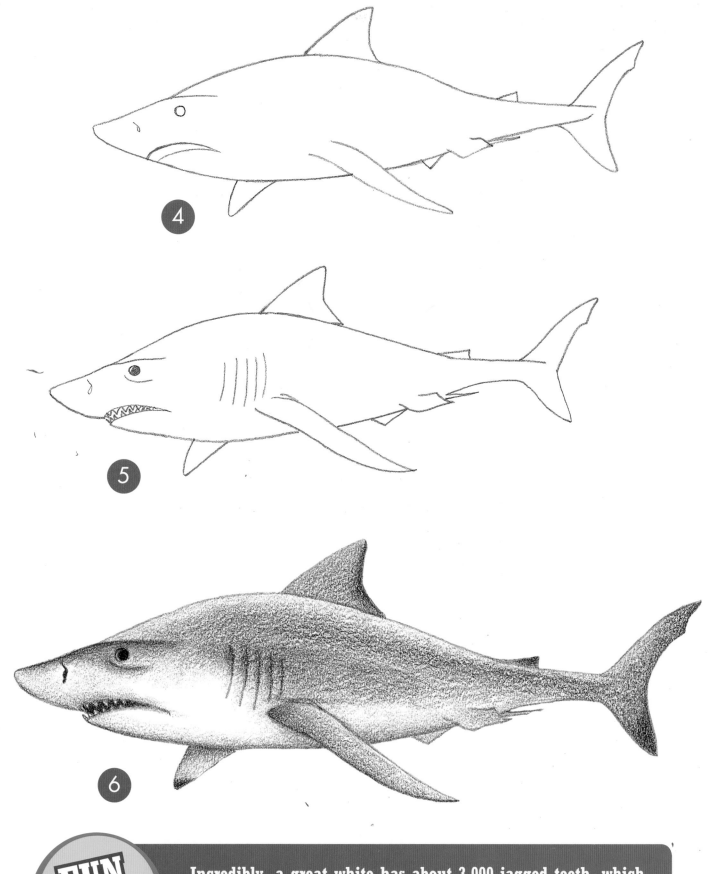

FUN FACT

Incredibly, a great white has about 3,000 jagged teeth, which are arranged in several rows. The shark uses only the first two rows for capturing prey; the rest of the teeth move into position when the front teeth are damaged or fall out.

Crocodile

Start with a thin **oval** body and a small **round** head—
then add the crocodile's long, strong tail and big, powerful jaws!

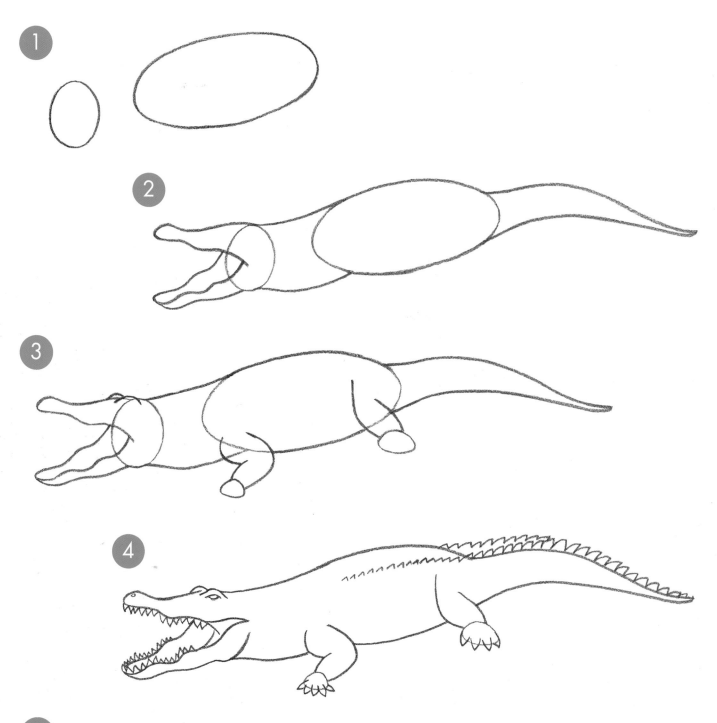

5

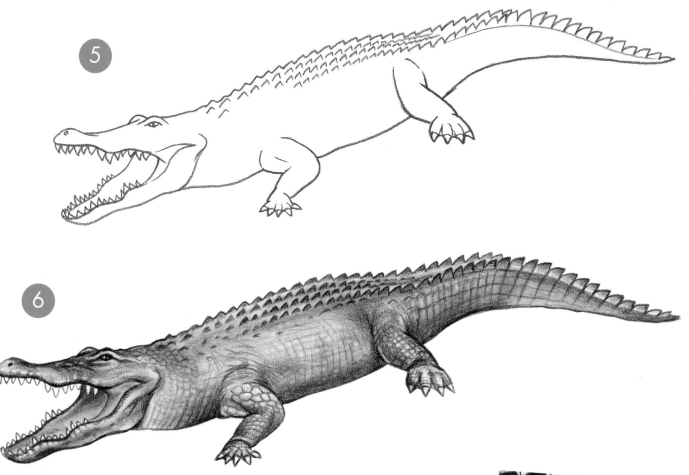

6

THE NOSE KNOWS

Can't tell the difference between the crocodile and the alligator? Check out the snout. The crocodile's snout is longer and V-shaped; the alligator's snout is wider and U-shaped.

FUN FACT

Crocodiles have five toes on their front feet, but only four toes on their back feet.

Sea Otter

This **cute** critter has **webbed** back feet, tiny ears, a foot-long tail, and thick brown fur.

Tiger

Every **big cat** has a large head and rounded ears. But a tiger also has *camouflaging* stripes that help this stand-out cat blend in!

Clownfish

A popular saltwater aquarium creature, the eye-catching clownfish sports bright gold bands of color.

1

2
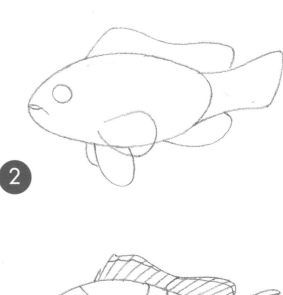

3
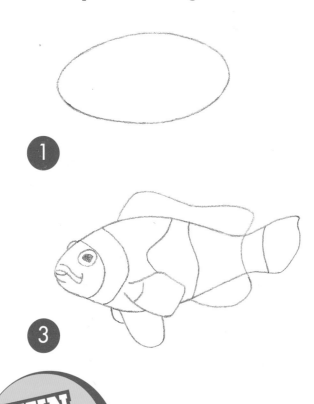

4

FUN FACT

The clownfish and sea anemone (an animal on the seafloor that resembles a flower) depend on one another for survival. After the anemone catches and eats a fish, the clownfish gets the leftovers that float nearby. In return, the clownfish protects the anemone from predators.

5

Lemur

Although its **long,** curving tail is the **ring-tailed** lemur's most striking feature, this animal is also known for its graceful, catlike posture.

Giraffe

With its **lanky** legs and long neck, the **towering** giraffe rises to claim the title of "tallest animal on Earth."

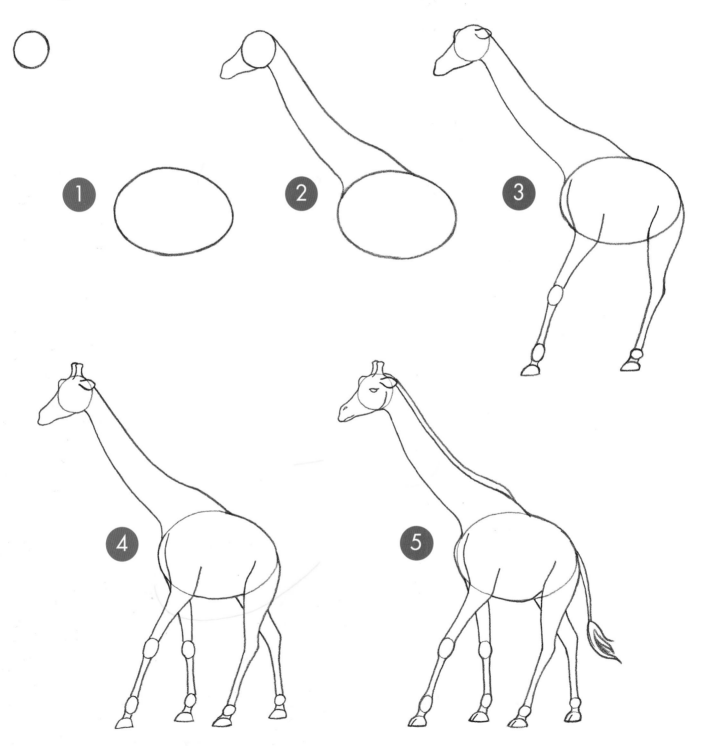

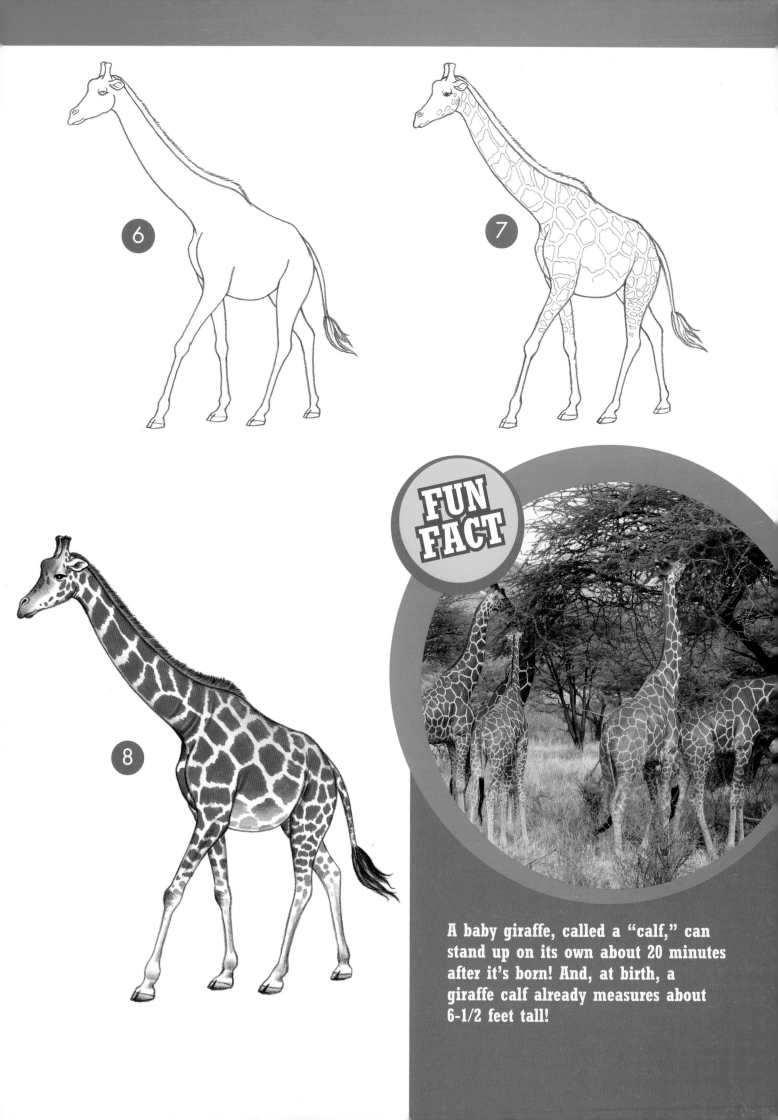

FUN FACT

A baby giraffe, called a "calf," can stand up on its own about 20 minutes after it's born! And, at birth, a giraffe calf already measures about 6-1/2 feet tall!

Dolphin

A **playful,** intelligent animal, the **dolphin** has a bottle-shaped beak and a happy expression that shows its friendly nature.

1

2

QUICK QUIZ!

Question: What do you call a group of dolphins?

The answer is at the bottom of the page.

3

Quick Quiz Answer: A pod. Sometimes these social creatures live in pods of up to several hundred dolphins.

34

4

5

FUN FACT

If you ever see a dolphin with just one eye open, chances are it's just sleeping! Because a dolphin can stay underwater for only 10 minutes before returning to the surface for air, it has to remain somewhat awake at all times. As a result, only one-half of the brain—and one eye—sleeps at one time!

Komodo

Don't let its **draggin'** belly fool you—the **large,** wrinkled, prehistoric-looking Komodo dragon is a swift runner and a fast climber.

FUN FACT

The natural habitat of the Komodo dragon is a group of four small islands in Indonesia. There are only about 5,000 Komodos in the wild today.

Armadillo

Oddly enough, the "nine-banded" armadillo can have from 8 to 10 bands around its body, making its tough armor more flexible.

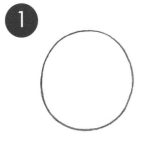

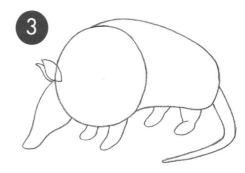

Many mammals give birth to multiple young, but only the nine-banded armadillo regularly produces them all from a single egg. The female always gives birth to quadruplets—that's four identical baby armadillos!

FOUR OF A KIND

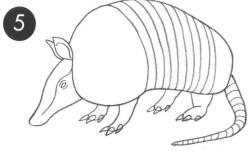

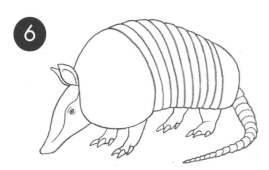

Sea Turtle

Begin drawing this **shelled** sea **creature** using a small circle for the head and an egg shape for the body.

1

2

3

FUN FACT

Sea turtles can feel vibrations in the water. This can help them locate food or steer clear of predators. They also have an excellent sense of smell.

4

5

SWELL SHELL

Contrary to what you may see in cartoons, a turtle can't crawl out of its shell, because the shell is part of its skeleton. Land turtles can pull their heads and limbs under their shells for protection, whereas sea turtles have streamlined shells and long, paddle-like flippers for faster swimming.

Animals in the Wild

Each animal has a natural environment, or *habitat*—whether a desert, forest, or water. To realistically portray your favorite animals, draw them in their own wild habitat, like this African grassland!

Underwater World

After you've learned to draw all the **fascinating** creatures in this book, try creating an awesome underwater scene!

Kangaroo

With a **thick,** powerful tail, **strong** hind legs, and huge rear feet, you can identify the kangaroo from a hop, skip, and a jump away!

5

6

For male kangaroos, kick boxing isn't a sport; it's a way of life. When fighting over mates, food, and resting spots, kangaroos will lock arms with each other, lean on their tails, and kick. The first kangaroo to get pushed over loses.

Walrus

The walrus is known for its **big, blubbery** body and its huge tusks, which can be up to 3 feet long!

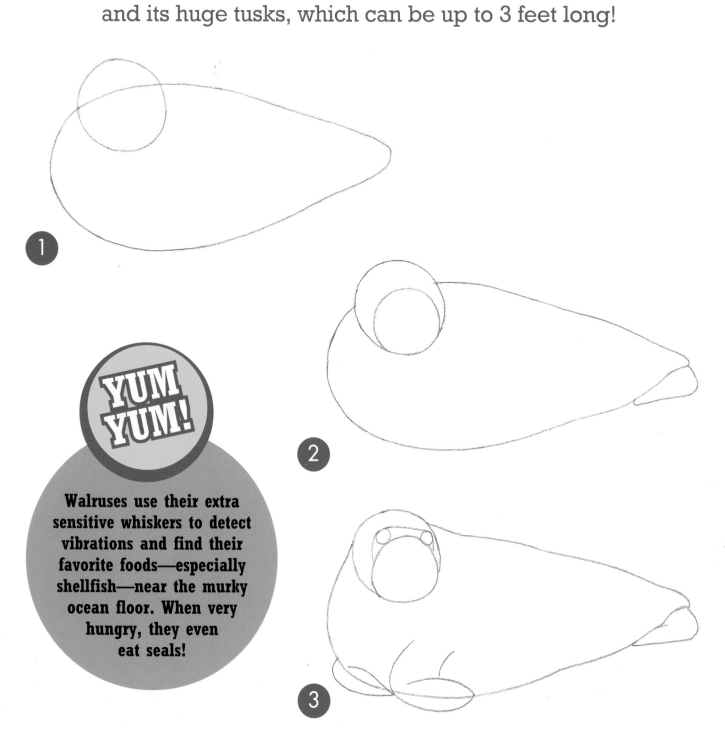

1

2

3

YUM YUM!

Walruses use their extra sensitive whiskers to detect vibrations and find their favorite foods—especially shellfish—near the murky ocean floor. When very hungry, they even eat seals!

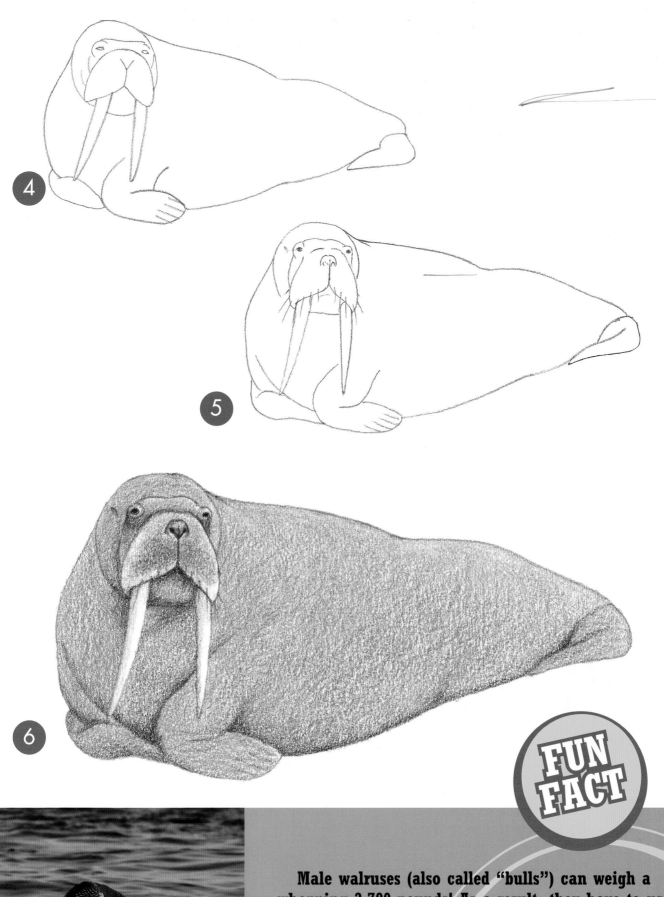

4

5

6

Male walruses (also called "bulls") can weigh a whopping 3,700 pounds! As a result, they have to use their strong tusks to help pull themselves out of the water and onto the ice. During mating season, the bulls also use their long tusks to protect their female "cows" from other male walruses.

Koala

This soft, **woolly** tree-dweller suspends its **short,** round body by clinging to eucalyptus trees—both its home and its food.

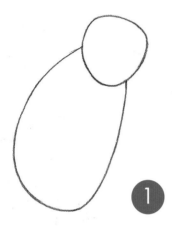

1

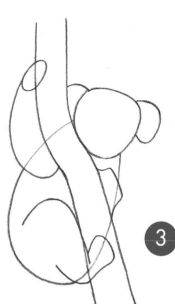

2

3

4

5

QUICK QUIZ!

Question: What do you call a baby koala?

The answer is at the bottom of the page.

Quick Quiz Answer: A joey.

6

Although eucalyptus leaves are the koala's primary source of food, this animal is a very picky eater. With over 600 eucalyptus varieties available, koalas eat only about 40 types and prefer just a select 10–12. As eucalyptus leaves don't provide much nutrition, koalas move slowly and sleep up to 20 hours a day to conserve energy.

FUN FACT

Tiger Shark

Why is the tiger shark so **easy** to **pick out** in a lineup? Because it has dark markings on its back that resemble a tiger's stripes!

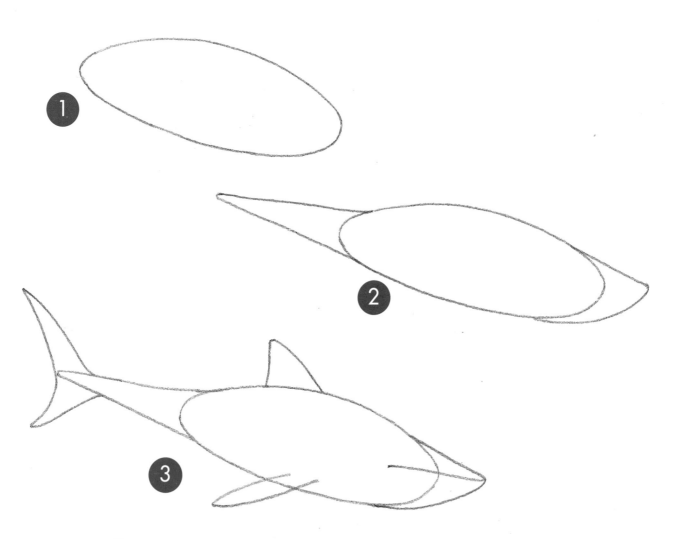

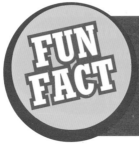

FUN FACT

Tiger sharks are known as the "wastebaskets of the sea" because they will eat just about anything, including people, old tires, and license plates!

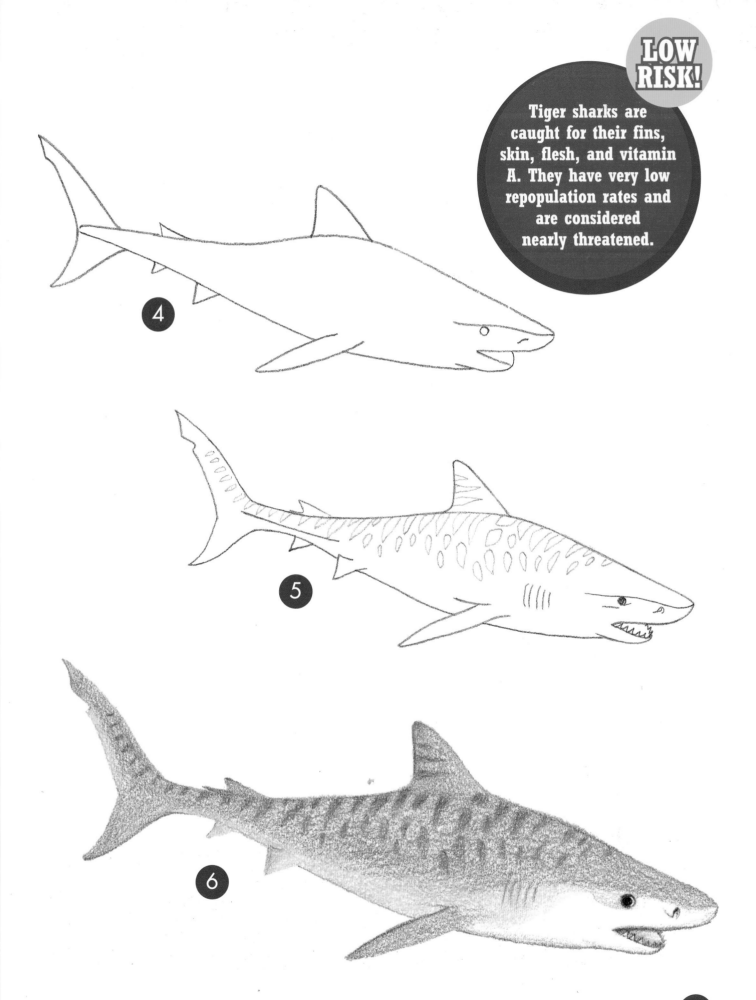

Tiger sharks are caught for their fins, skin, flesh, and vitamin A. They have very low repopulation rates and are considered nearly threatened.

4

5

6

Swordfish

This fish's long, sharp **bill** resembles a **sword,** creating a streamlined shape that's perfect for speedy swimming!

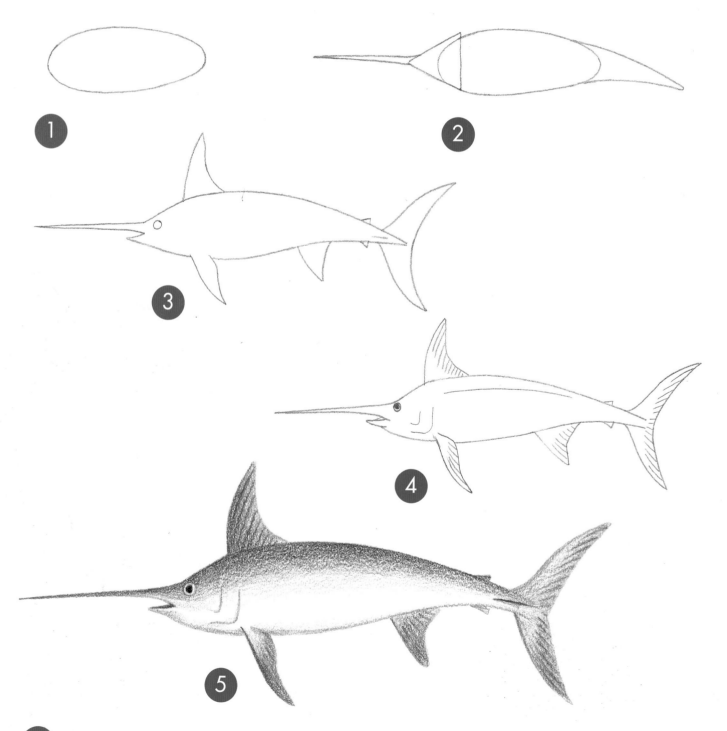

1

2

3

4

5

Orangutan

Every orangutan has a **bare** face, **round** eyes, and small ears, but only the male has large, round cheek pads and a long, hairy beard.

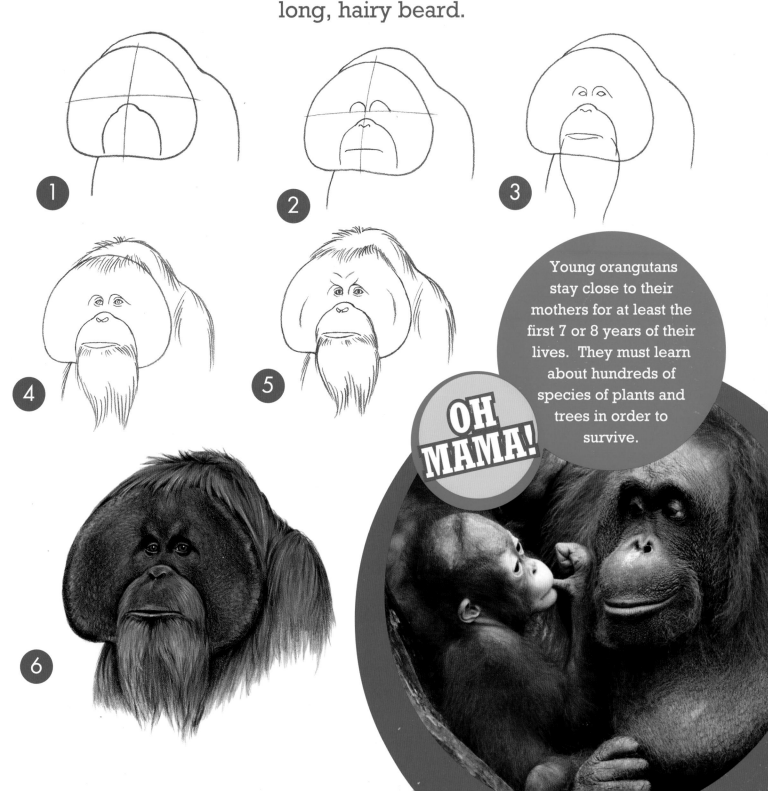

Young orangutans stay close to their mothers for at least the first 7 or 8 years of their lives. They must learn about hundreds of species of plants and trees in order to survive.

OH MAMA!

Rhinoceros

The **short** legs of this white rhino support its **bulky** body, and it uses its two curved, triangular-shaped horns to dig for food and defend itself!

1

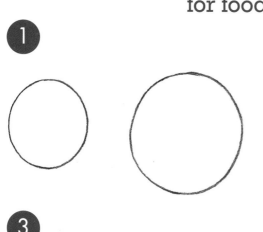

2

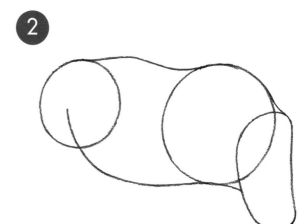

3

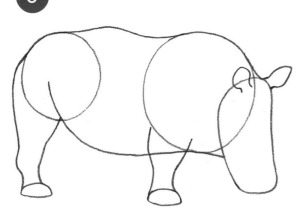

4

In Africa, the white rhino population suffers due to habitat loss. But illegal hunting (called "poaching") is also a threat to this rhino's survival.

HIGH RISK!

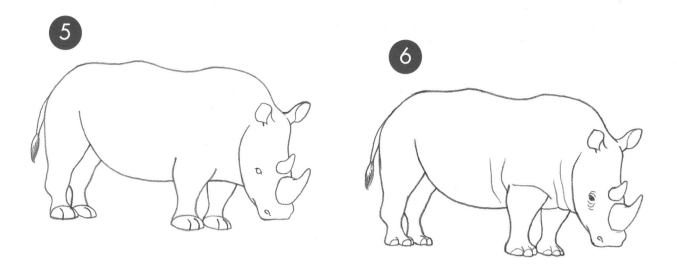

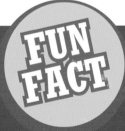

Why name a gray rhino "white"? Blame it on a misunderstanding. The Dutch word for wide—weit—is pronounced "white." Weit was meant to describe the rhino's wide, square muzzle—not its color. It's no coincidence that this animal is also called the "square-lipped" rhino.

Orca

The **black** and **white** markings on an orca—
or "killer whale"—make this amazing animal easy
to identify!

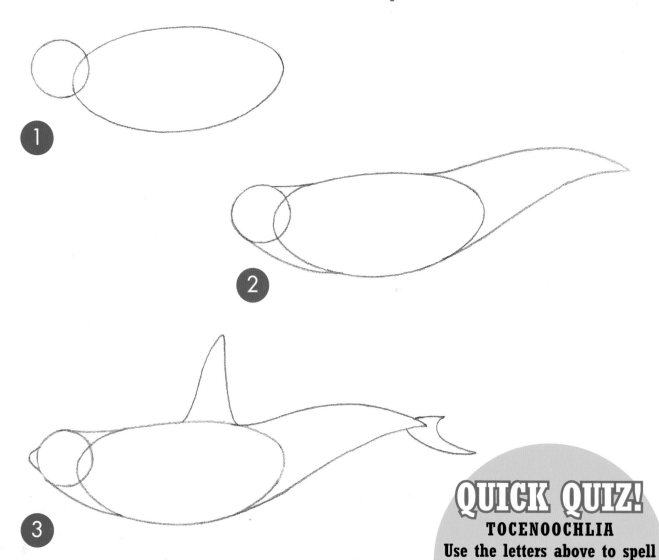

1

2

3

QUICK QUIZ!

TOCENOOCHLIA
Use the letters above to spell
out the word that describes
how toothed whales detect
the objects around them.
See answer below.

ECHOLOCATION
Quick Quiz Answer:

66

The orca is an extremely skilled hunter, giving it the nickname "killer whale." But although it feeds on a wide range of prey—from small fish to blue whales—a wild orca has never been known to kill a human.

Tapir

What's **black** and **white** with a long curved snout? The Malayan tapir! This "living fossil" has looked exactly the same for 30 million years!

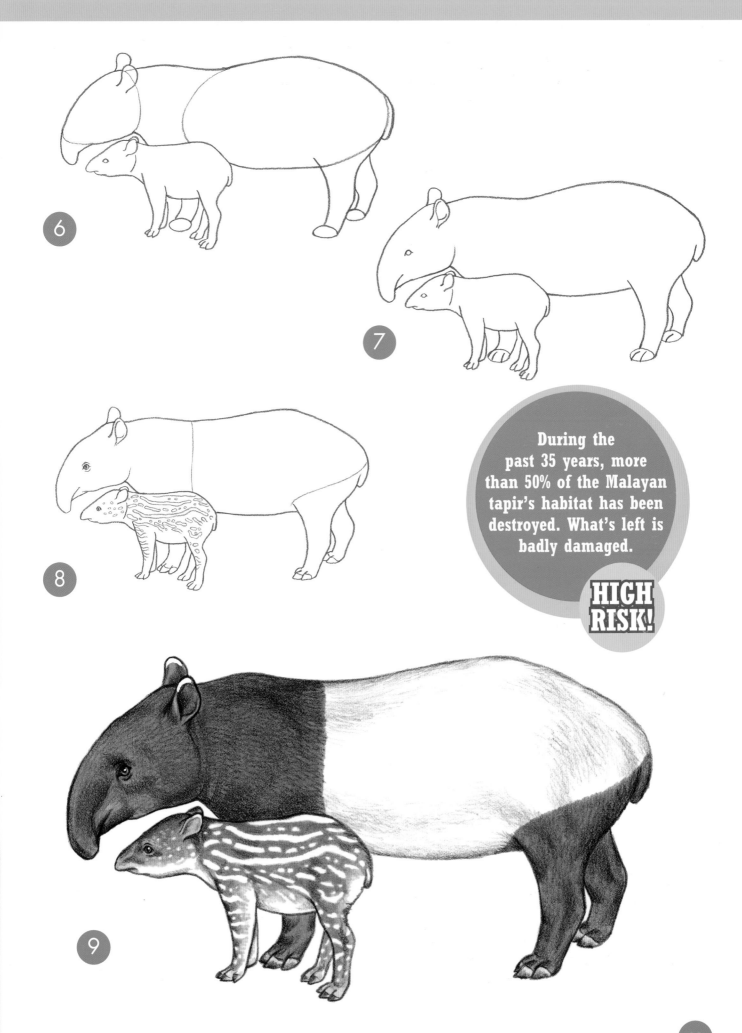

6

7

8

During the
past 35 years, more
than 50% of the Malayan
tapir's habitat has been
destroyed. What's left is
badly damaged.

**HIGH
RISK!**

9

Okapi

Its **stripes** make the okapi look like a zebra, but this **tall,** two-toned animal has the long legs and flexible neck of a giraffe.

AT RISK!

The okapi is quickly losing its habitat to human farms, roads, and homes. And this animal is also hunted as a source of food.

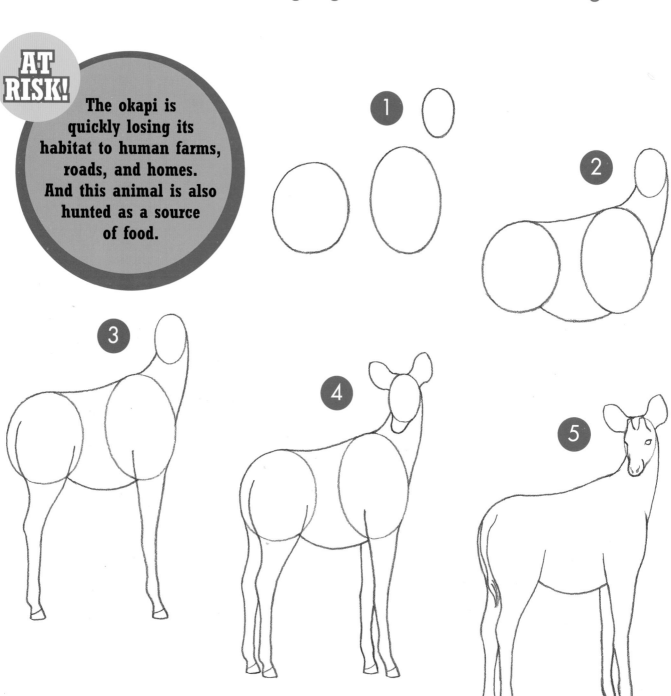

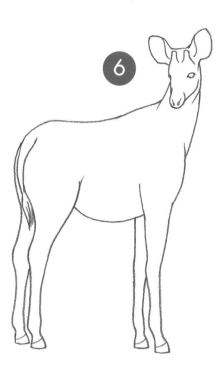

6

7

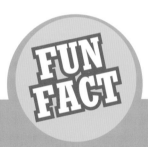

FUN FACT

The okapi lives only in the tropical forests of north-eastern Zaire, on the African continent, where it hides itself in the thick vegetation. A very shy animal, the okapi is rarely seen in the wild. Because of this, the okapi was thought to be a "forest zebra" until 1900, when it was finally recognized as its own unique species of animal. The okapi has no relation to the zebra, but it is the only known relative of the giraffe.

8

Octopus

The octopus has a **soft,** oval body and **eight** arms covered with bubblelike suction cups.

Quick Quiz Answer: True! An octopus can mimic the colors and patterns of its surroundings.

4

QUICK QUIZ!

TRUE or FALSE?
An octopus can hide
in plain sight of
dangerous predators.

The answer is at the bottom
of the opposite page.

5

FUN FACT

This animal doesn't just
have multiple arms—it
has multiple hearts too!
An octopus has three
hearts: two for pumping
blood through its gills to
get oxygen, and one for
pumping blood through
its entire body.

Zebra

From its **black** muzzle to the tips of its **long** ears, the zebra's face is covered in narrow stripes; its body and mane have broader stripes.

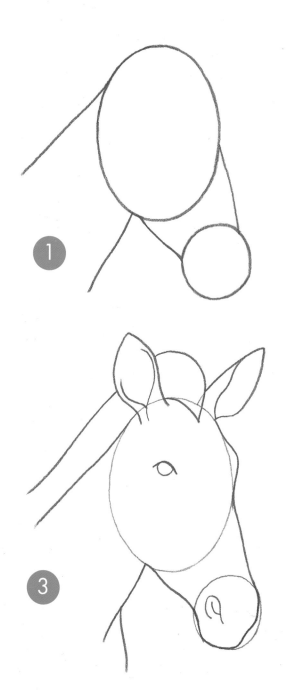

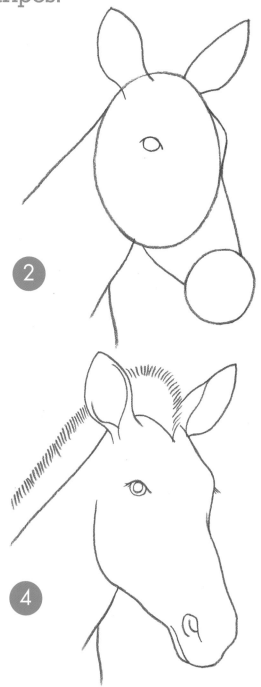

5

6

Experts aren't exactly sure why zebras have stripes, but they think that the markings serve some sort of purpose. The stripes might help the animals recognize other members of their herd, regulate temperature, or confuse predators.

Seahorse

This **critter** has a **horselike** head; a spiky, S-shaped body; and a long, curled tail.

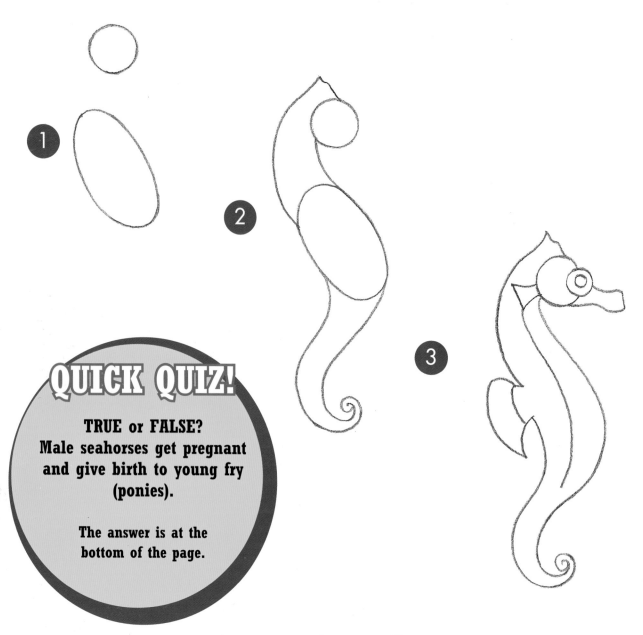

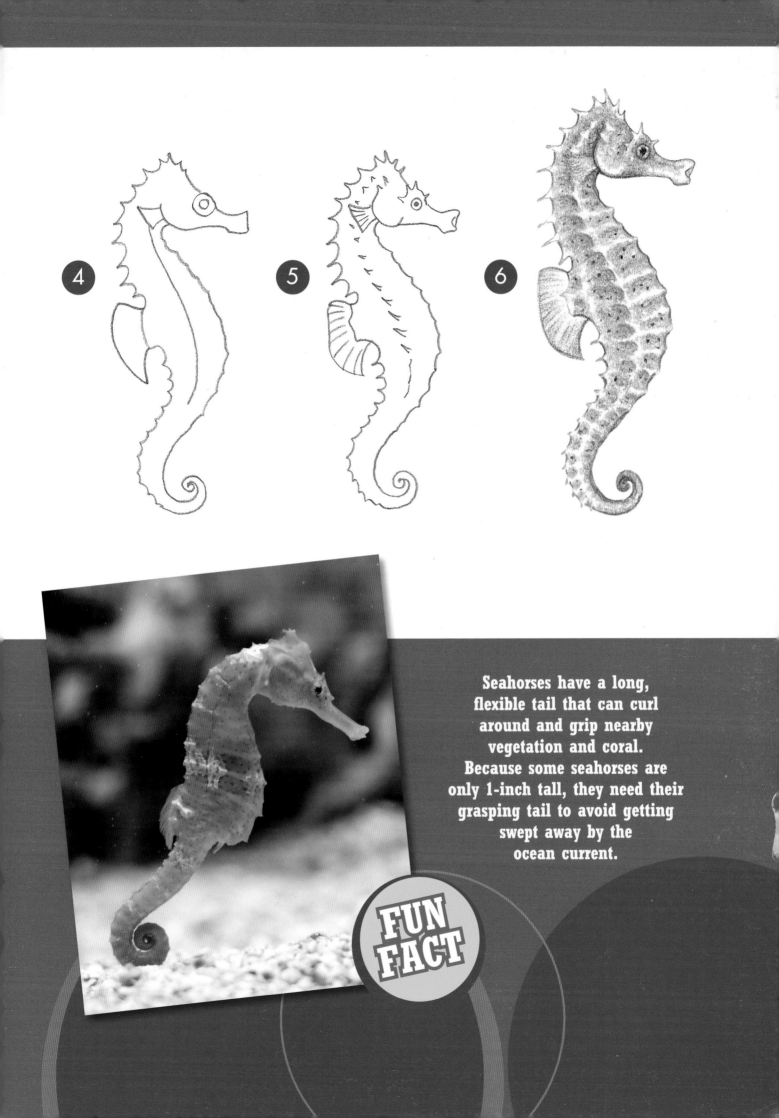

4 5 6

Seahorses have a long, flexible tail that can curl around and grip nearby vegetation and coral. Because some seahorses are only 1-inch tall, they need their grasping tail to avoid getting swept away by the ocean current.

FUN FACT

Glossary

Amphibious (AM-fib-ee-iss) - To be able to live on land and in water.

Ampullae (AM-pew-lay) - Special organs on sharks that can detect electrical fields around prey.

Camouflage (CAM-o-flaj) - To hide by blending in with the surroundings.

Cartilage (CAR-ti-lij) - A tough, flexible tissue that is softer than bone and found in sharks.

Crustacean (crus-TAY-shin) - An animal that usually lives in water and has a hard outer shell and several pairs of legs.

Echolocation (E-ko-lo-cay-shin) - How dolphins and whales locate objects by sending out sounds and studying their echoes.

Exoskeleton (EK-so-ske-le-tin) - A hard, outer covering, such as the shell of a turtle or lobster.

Extinct (EK-stinct) - No longer living or existing.

Habitat (HAB-i-tat) - Where an animal lives, such as the ocean or desert.

Mammal (MA-mol) - A warm-blooded animal that has hair, gives birth to live young, and feeds its young milk, such as a human or bear.

Predator (PRE-da-tur) - An animal that kills and eats other animals.

Tentacle (TEN-ta-kul) - A long, flexible organ that grows near the mouth of an animal, such as a jellyfish or octopus, used for feeding or grasping.